THE S WORD

THE S WORD

GR8 RELATIONSHIPS

EQUIP PRESS

Colorado Springs

THE S WORD

Published by Equip Press, Colorado Springs, CO

First Edition: 2023
The S Word / (GR8 Relationships)
Paperback ISBN: 978-1-958585-70-2
eBook ISBN: 978-1-958585-71-9

EQUIP PRESS
Colorado Springs

CONTENTS

INTRODUCTION

The S-Word?!? Did you pick this book up wondering which *S*-word we are talking about? Some expletives might come to mind.

Read on. You may be surprised . . . and besides, we know you are curious.

Cue the drum roll.

We are talking about something that people struggle with in their relationships with each other and with God. Submission. Are you cringing? At least it wasn't a bad word. Or maybe submission is a bad word to you. And now you may be wondering, "Why is submission important?" Isn't that an old archaic idea in a relationship?

Let's take a look and see. What we know is that submission is a biblical principle so we know it is important to see what scriptures say. Let start with looking at what Ephesians says:

> . . . *be filled with the Spirit, speaking to one*
> *another in psalms and hymns and spiritual*
> *songs, singing and making melody in your heart*
> *to the Lord, giving thanks always for all things*

to God the Father in the name of our Lord Jesus
Christ, submitting to one another in the fear
of God.

Ephesians 5:18-21, NKJV

It seems that everyone wants to stay away from submission, right? Submission is not something people want to talk about. And unfortunately, it seems that submission is primarily a topic when dealing with women in the church. After all, the word of God says that a woman is to submit.

Well, you will read about submission here, but it will be a different, clearly biblical view. Actually, submission involves all people and all parts of life because that is the way God designed it.

The difficulty with submission is that we make everything about *ME*. As you have read in this book series the *Flashing ME* presents a problem in relationships among our friends, family, spouses, and peers—as well as God. If you think about the opposite of the *Flashing ME*, it is pursuing the best for others. When you pursue the best for others you submit to what is best for them instead of what is best for you. In choosing what is best for others or pursuing *their* best, you really benefit yourself, because your relationships can be stronger and deeper. You might even find less conflict in relationships.

Truly, as we read in the Ephesians passage above, I am to submit to you; you are to submit to me. I am to submit to others in the body of Christ and they are to submit to me. Everyone is to submit to each other. We do this in the fear of God! That should be impetus enough for all of us to focus on submitting to each other and to Him, no matter what the situation is.

All of this will impact relationships, especially marriages. It will impact your family. It will impact the church. It will impact work. And if you do not do what is stated in Ephesians 5:21, you will impact all those relationships negatively, because without submission everything is about *ME*.

Unfortunately, submission is often discussed like a scene from a children's playground. One of the children starts trying to dominate and control the others.

Then a one child says, "Stop it! You can't treat me like that!"

And the child that was acting out says, "Why not?"

And the first child says, "Cause my dad says so!"

Submission is seldom seen as something positive. It is like the child in the playground, but invoking God instead, "You'd better submit, because God said so!"

It happens that way because submission is not defined with the image of God in mind.

Read that sentence again!

Going back to Ephesians 5:21, the words *fear of God* are especially important, because the phrase is most often translated as reverential awe.

I am not a Greek or a Hebrew scholar, but I do have good resources. They show *fear of God* in Ephesians 5:21, to mean *dread, terror*. We should have a dread, a terror of God if we don't submit to Him. This gives a bit of a different view of the fear of the Lord!

Now, what do you think is driving most people to define fear as reverential awe?

Fear gets distorted when you only see God through the lens of love. Yes, He is love, but He is more than that, and so is love. Too many people see God as a vending machine in the sky. They think things like, "He's supposed to treat me well and give me everything that I'm supposed to have."

That's the relational component of God, but if you go back to the *Image of God* there is a power component, too! When the word *fear* is stated here, God is talking about His power. In other words, "Pay attention to this. This is not my relational side that I am showing you right now. It is my power."

Yes, He is our friend. He is our father. That whole relational side is true, but that is not all that Ephesians 5:21 is about.

He is powerful, He is high and lifted up as you see in Isaiah.

> . . . *the High and Lofty One Who inhabits eternity* . . .

Isaiah 57:15, NKJV

Or, like the picture Ezekiel shares in chapter one.

. . . a whirlwind. . .a great cloud with raging fire engulfing itself. . .

Ezekiel 1:4-28, NKJV

And, as you read further you see that God is above all this amazing power.

And above the firmament over their heads was the likeness of a throne, in appearance like a sapphire stone; on the likeness of the throne was a likeness with the appearance of a man high above it.

Ezekiel 1:26, NKJV

God is high above everything! The throne is magnificent enough; but the One Who is on the throne is far above the throne! Those pictures are the reason why, as you read in the Bible that people fall down before God, flat on their face – "Oh WOW! That is God! Oh no!"

What power! What unbelievable power! Unbelievable!

So, when Paul tells us to submit ". . . in the fear of God . . ." I do not accept that as reverential awe. It is better to see that as dread and terror. God is not playing games with anything that He says in His Word and this passage (like others) is even more important, since it states, "in the fear of God."

Yes, I do understand that reverential awe helps demonstrate the grace and freedom aspect. It is also important to understand that God's boundaries, when violated, create bad consequences for us. So please do not dilute the "fear of God" into something cuddly and warm! If you do dilute the fear of God and do not submit, James 4:1 will mark your relationships.

> *Where do wars and fights come from among you?*
> *Do they not come from your desires for pleasure*
> *that war in your members?*

James 4:1, NKJV

If you do not submit to others, you're going to be fighting with them because your *ME* is flashing. You want to be the one that is right and admired. And God says, "No, that isn't the way I want it. I want you seek the bottom, not the top." That is the reason this statement is so true and good: Fighting for the top is selfishness, for the bottom is serving. Submission asks us to transform into serving mode, away from and out of the selfish mode.

Submission is not a "four-letter word" that we should not say; it is foundational to relationships, and it starts with our relationship with almighty God. If we choose not to recognize Him as almighty and powerful and instead *soft-sell* submitting to Him, we do a great disservice to all our relationships. Step one is submitting to Him, even when we don't want to, which leads to submitting to others.

You may think, "Well wait a minute, what if I submit to others and they don't reciprocate?" The fact is you can't control someone else's behavior, only influence it. So, if you live a life of submission, you may influence others and thus influence their relationship with you and whoever else they are in relationship with. But others treating you well is not the issue. Obeying God, walking with Him, and becoming more like Jesus is the issue. Jesus always submitted to the Father and served others, including you and me.

<u>REFLECTIVE QUESTIONS</u>

1. Think about how you have thought about the word submission in the past. What words come to mind?
2. What new perspective did you gain about submission from reading the Introduction to this book?
3. Why is it important to think about God's power when considering what submission means in your life?
4. How will this Introduction impact your relationships moving forward?

SUBMISSION DEFINED

L et's dig a little deeper into what submission means. We'll start with the very nature of mankind.

Left to your sin nature, you will constantly want to be in control, to be in charge. You are not being submissive, but more likely telling people what to do. Obviously, that is not how submission works. Submission helps you pursue the best for others. It is the component of relationships where you serve others. In order to understand why this is true you need a good definition of submission.

When you look at the Greek word *hupotássō* that translates to submit, it means the following.

- To place in order
- To place under in an orderly fashion

When used in Ephesians 5:22, it is *hupotássomai,* which further means:

- To subject oneself
- Place oneself in submission

It is a choice to make a personal subjection to another person. The military provides a clear picture of what the word means. In the military there are officers and those *under* the officers; or, commanders and the people under the commanders. The officers or commanders are under the ultimate leader.

The non-military usage is similar. Consider the hierarchy in your job or a corporation. You may be a training professional in your company. People may report to you, but you have a boss who has a boss. If all of you were just doing your own thing it would be chaos. Being part of a team and ultimately part of a company department, you have someone to submit to. That doesn't mean you just blindly do what you are told to do, because you have something valuable to contribute. However, you yield yourself to the authority or will of another because you want to be in alignment with your organization and the team you are a part of in that organization. So, submission means to line up underneath. Why? For *order,* or to create order. Think about how that might work in your current work situation.

When you are in a relationship and following this idea of submission, you are willing to line yourself up underneath another person as a means of supporting them and maintaining order. This is not all there is to submission, but it is a critical use of submission.

Notice how this works with love. When you pursue the best for someone, patiently, kindly, sacrificially, and unconditionally you willingly line up underneath them.

All of God's Word fits together and this is just one piece of what makes relationships work best.

Please keep in mind that submission is for everyone, not just for women! Remember Ephesians 5:21 states, "Submitting yourselves one to another."

So men, please, never talk to your wife about submission if you do not understand it yourself. Until you learn how to submit to your boss the way God wants you to and submit to authorities the way God wants you to, then please do not try to get anyone to submit to you, much less your wife.

A simple, workable definition of submission is:

An internal, voluntary act of the will to yield to another.

That means you choose to submit. No one can make you submit.

Here are four Bible verses that provide the practical application of submission in your daily life.

> *. . . that you also submit to such, and to everyone who works and labors with us.*

1 Corinthians 16:16, NKJV

Therefore submit yourselves to every ordinance of man for the Lord's sake, whether to the king as supreme, or to governors, as to those who are sent by him for the punishment of evildoers and for the praise of those who do good.

1 Peter 2:13-14, NKJV

Likewise you younger people, submit yourselves to your elders. Yes, all of you be submissive to one another, and be clothed with humility, for "God resists the proud, but gives grace to the humble.

1 Peter 5:5, NKJV

Obey those who rule over you, and be submissive, for they watch out for your souls, as those who must give account. Let them do so with joy and not with grief, for that would be unprofitable for you.

Hebrews 13:17, NKJV

Many other scriptures are just as clear and practical. They can impact your daily living. God's Word clearly wants you to submit. Why? Because this is the way the body of Christ works best. God wants each member of the body serving the others, thinking of others as more important than themselves rather than their *ME* flashing all the time. God wants you to submit to others in the fear of God because that makes the body healthy.

Submission Displays God's Image

Submission is actually displayed between the Father, Son, and the Holy Spirit. Let's look at submission with regard to the image of God. What could be a more important topic than the image of God?

When you apply the image of God to what you study in the Bible, you gain new insight into that area of study. As you study submission, two approaches tend to show up. One is authority and submission, and the other is mutual submission. Authority and submission might be obvious. It is the powerful element of the image of God. Mutual submission is the relational aspect of the image of God.

Submission is a word that describes how people relate to each other, but every relationship has a power element and relating element. For submission, the authority and submission approach concerns *order* in the relationship. On the other hand, the mutual submission approach provides the *harmony* or relating aspect in the relationship.

You reduce chaos in the relationship when you have order, and you reduce the flashing *ME* in a relationship when you have harmony. Order is an impersonal structure and harmony is a personal structure.

The problem with discussing submission is people only want to talk about one side or the other. Mostly, people want to talk about mutual submission. They only want to talk about how we are supposed to be mutually submitting one to another in the fear of God.

The relational side of submission is definitely important; however, the power, order, or authority and submission attribute is equally important. Both must be considered because Christians are supposed to voluntarily put themselves under authority and carry the burdens for others. When you do it that way, with order and harmony, you practice submission in a way that fits the image of God. And that is exactly the point!

Submission Displays the Mind of Christ

It is easy to shy away from or ignore submission because we call it the *S Word*. People do not want to talk about submission, because it seems too controversial. And, of course, when it involves women to men or wife to husband, "Oh, don't touch that one! That's not politically correct!"

This powerful word has such a bad reputation, despite the fact that it plugs directly into the solution for every relationship. The minute you submit the way God wants you to, it not only demonstrates the mind of Christ, but it also completely cancels out the *Flashing ME*.

The mind of Jesus Christ is clearly shown in the scripture below from Philippians.

> *Let nothing be done through selfish ambition or conceit, but in lowliness of mind let each esteem others better than himself. Let each of you look out not only for his own interests, but also for the interests of others. Let this mind be in you which was also in Christ Jesus, who, being in the form of God, did not consider it robbery to be equal with God, but made Himself of no reputation, taking the form of a bondservant, and coming in the likeness of men. And being found in appearance as a man, He humbled Himself and became obedient to the point of death, even the death of the cross.*

Philippians 2:3-8, NKJV

When you have the mind of Christ, you think of others as more important than yourself. You put their interests in front of yours as you can see in verses three and four. You can see in verses five through eight that the mind of Christ lowers you to sacrifice for others and submit to the needs of others. That is exactly how Christ wants you to think about relationships.

Christ submitted to our need. Christ has all authority. Everything lines up underneath Him. He is the authority. He provides the *order* for the entire universe. He is in charge, but notice what He did.

He took His authority and said, "I'm going to create harmony between Me and you. I have all authority. I can order anything to be the way I want it, so I am going to provide the path for you to have *harmony* with Me." So you can see the two elements of submission in those verses.

Submission is always voluntary for both order and harmony. You will either voluntarily line yourself underneath someone to support them, even if you are the leader, or you will focus on whether they are lining up underneath you. When you lead, you use both elements of submission to create both order and harmony. When you submit in this way you demonstrate love and pursue their best patiently, kindly, sacrificially, and unconditionally.

If you do not have the foundation of love, submission will be exceedingly difficult. So, I believe love comes first. It is the highest of all the values. And when you submit with the correct intent of your heart, then you practice the love of God with others.

Submission Scenario

In the scenario below, think about the following attributes of submission. At the end of the scenario, answer the questions regarding the attributes of submission.

Submission Attributes

- Submission is a voluntary act, it cannot be forced on someone.
- Submission reflects the authority of God's order.
- Submission applies to everyone in the Body of Christ. We submit to each other.
- Submission reduces or removes the *Flashing ME.*

Scenario

Amos and Deborah have been married for 16 years. Both are in their mid-40s. They do not have children, but have four Golden Retrievers that they consider as kids. Amos is a Marketing Director for a Fortune 500 company and Deborah is an attorney for a Real Estate firm. Deborah travels about 50 percent of the time. Amos does not have to travel for business.

When Deborah is traveling, Amos has the burden of going home several times a day to take care of the dogs. Deborah is the true dog-lover in the family, but Amos doesn't want them destroying their home. Amos is more meticulous about their home and the order in the house.

They attend a small church near their home, and both are involved in small group Bible studies. Amos is more regular in attendance to his Bible study than Deborah. She has complained many times that the leader of the Bible study has no clue what it is like to have a high-powered job that requires so much travel. Her Bible study leader, Tiffany, is a stay-at-home mom with four children. Tiffany has never worked outside the home and her husband brings in a high-paying income as a medical doctor. He is gone a lot due to the requirements of his medical practice, but it does not concern Tiffany since she can hire domestic helpers if she needs to. Deborah just doesn't feel she can respect Tiffany, because she is too naïve.

Amos, on the other hand, speaks very highly of the leader of his group, John, who is a small business owner. He doesn't always agree with John's opinion, yet considers how what John says might apply to him. Amos is always trying to see how he can help and support the men in his Bible study, whether it is with their work or personal walk with the Lord.

Many times Amos has suggested to Deborah that the Bible study is a group where Deborah doesn't have to feel the need to control things and be in charge. He suggests that it's a different scenario than her job, where she must represent and fight for her company as a lawyer. He encourages her to try not to be in control, but just look at how she can respect her Bible leader, even though she does not have the same background.

Amos is more of the home manager than Deborah since she is not at home as much. Amos is very methodical about everything in the home. Deborah gets a little frustrated with Amos because he expects the house to be totally neat, with nothing out of order, and wants Deborah to follow more of a set schedule. Deborah does not use an alarm when she is home because she wants to stick to her circadian rhythms for health reasons. She feels like he is trying to force his way of doing things on her. They do not spend much quiet time together because each one is pursuing their own career and they have totally different personality styles.

Amos feels like she does not respect his need for the house to be neat. Often she can't find something because she didn't put it where it belonged. He feels like she creates her own chaos by not being more methodical about putting things away or leaving the house early enough to make it to a meeting, so she's always rushing out the door. Amos also has most of the responsibility for taking care of the dogs and he feels like she could help more, because she's the dog lover in the first place.

Scenario Questions

1. Submission is a voluntary act, it cannot be forced on someone.

_____

_____

_____

_____

2. How does this attribute apply to the scenario?

_____

_____

_____

3. Submission reflects the authority of God's order.

_____

_____

_____

4. How does this attribute apply to the scenario?

_____

_____

_____

5. Submission applies to everyone in the Body of Christ. We must all submit to each other.

_____

_____

_____

6. How does this attribute apply to the scenario?

_____

_____

_____

7. Submission reduces or removes the Flashing
   ME.

_____

_____

_____

_____

8. How does this attribute apply to the scenario?

_____

_____

_____

_____

REFLECTIVE QUESTIONS

- Based on this definition of submission, what changes can you make in your personal relationships? *Submission means: An internal, voluntary act of the will to yield to another. That means you choose to submit. No one can make you submit.*

_____

_____

_____

_____

- Based on the fact that submission has a relating element that creates harmony and a power element that creates order, think about some non-family relationships you have. Which element do you need to improve in that relationship? Why? (what will be your expected result?)

_____

_____

_____

_____

MUTUAL SUBMISSION

Submission is a component of all healthy relationships. The easiest one to apply it to is marriage, but it also applies to work, and friend and family relationships. Applied correctly in marriages, submission provides order for the marriage and establishes harmony between husband and wife. Unfortunately, many people apply submission in marriage to women more than men.

The apostle Paul speaks of how submission and love apply to various relationships as listed below.

- Ephesians 5:21: Mutual submission as the standard for all believers:

  . . . submitting to one another in the fear of God

  Ephesians 5:21, NKJV

The passage that follows, Ephesians 5:22-31, mutual submission and love is the standard for the marriage:

  Wives, submit to your own husbands, as to the Lord. For the husband is head of the wife, as

also Christ is head of the church; and He is the
Savior of the body. Therefore, just as the church is
subject to Christ, so let the wives be to their own
husbands in everything.

Husbands, love your wives, just as Christ also
loved the church and gave Himself for her, that
He might [a]sanctify and cleanse her with the
washing of water by the word, that He might
present her to Himself a glorious church, not
having spot or wrinkle or any such thing, but
that she should be holy and without blemish. So
husbands ought to love their own wives as
their own bodies; he who loves his wife loves
himself. For no one ever hated his own flesh,
but nourishes and cherishes it, just as the
Lord does the church. For we are members of His
body, [b]of His flesh and of His bones. "For this
reason a man shall leave his father and mother
and be joined to his wife, and the two shall
become one flesh.

Ephesians 5:22-31

• Continuing through Ephesians 6:1-4, mutual
submission is for parents and children – the
family:

Children, obey your parents in the Lord, for this
is right. "Honor your father and mother," which

*is the first commandment with promise: "that
it may be well with you and you may live long
on the earth." And you, fathers, do not provoke
your children to wrath, but bring them up in the
training and admonition of the Lord*

Ephesians 6:1-4, NKJV

- And in Ephesians 6:5-9, mutual submission
  applies to the workplace:

*Bondservants, be obedient to those who are your
masters according to the flesh, with fear and
trembling, in sincerity of heart, as to Christ;
not with eyeservice, as men-pleasers, but as
bondservants of Christ, doing the will of God
from the heart, with goodwill doing service,
as to the Lord, and not to men, knowing that
whatever good anyone does, he will receive the
same from the Lord, whether he is a slave or free.*

*And you, masters, do the same things to them,
giving up threatening, knowing that [a]your
own Master also is in heaven, and there is no
partiality with Him.*

Ephesians 6:5-9, NKJV

Marriage and Family

Many men might have difficulty understanding how they are supposed to submit to their wives. Some might even say, "Huh? She's supposed to submit to me!"

While that is true, God asks him to submit to his wife as well. The notion of husband and wife submitting to each other can be misguided because some see husband and wife as equal rulers in the family, which is not what God wants. Mutual submission without regard for authority and order will drive a marriage into a ditch. So, as we talk about mutual submission in marriage (or any relationship for that matter) we do not dismiss God's desire for authority and order.

Let's look at a practical example. A husband submits to his wife by doing what God asks the husband to do for her. He submits to her need for safety and security when he loves her, cherishes her, develops her, sacrifices for her, protects her, provides for her, and preserves her.

When you do those things, as a husband, you submit to meeting her needs. When God asks you as a husband to love your wife unconditionally, you practice mutual submission, putting yourself underneath her to serve her as any great leader and husband would do. Just like Jesus did for you!

As a husband, if you are not doing the things listed above, then you are not submitting to her need to feel secure. That is a need she has as a woman. This is not limited to providing money, food, clothes, and shelter.

She also has a need for a loving relationship. With mutual submission, you submit to your wife by doing what God asks you to do in order to meet her relational needs. Let's see what 1 Peter says about this.

> *Husbands, likewise, dwell with them with understanding, giving honor to the wife, as to the weaker vessel, and as being heirs together of the grace of life, that your prayers may not be hindered.*

1 Peter 3:7, NKJV

The context of this verse is unjust suffering as we see in 1 Peter 2:20-22

> *. . . But when you do good and suffer, if you take it patiently, this is commendable before God. For to this you were called, because Christ also suffered for us, leaving us an example, that you should follow His steps:*
>
> *"Who committed no sin, Nor was deceit found in His mouth"*

1 Peter 2:20-22, NKJV

So, 1 Peter 3:7 says that even if your wife is treating you badly for doing right things, stay with her, dwell with her in an understanding way. This is honorable to God. It is submitting to her needs. In a marriage relationship the husband submits to the wife and the wife submits to the husband.

> *Wives, submit to your own husbands, as to the Lord.*

Ephesians 5:22, NKJV

Mutual submission supports relating to each other in marriage and authority maintains order in the relationship.

Submission in Families

Submission goes beyond marriage relationships. It is part of every relationship including family, work, and church. Submission in the family follows the same principles as you just read about for the marriage. Ephesians 6 is a key passage to consider.

> *Children, obey your parents in the Lord, for this is right. "Honor your father and mother," which is the first commandment with promise: "that it may be well with you and you may live long on the earth." And you, fathers, do not provoke your children to wrath, but bring them up in the training and admonition of the Lord.*

Ephesians 6:1-4, NKJV

This truth has stayed constant from the Old Testament to the New, because the passage above references Exodus 20:12. Parents can create problems for their children when they triangle them.

The issue here is similar to that of a husband and wife. How do parents submit to their children? It is right there in those verses. When you teach, correct, and develop them you are actually submitting to their need to be raised in God's truth, in a way that will save them from big problems.

Secondly, it says, ". . . fathers, do not provoke your children to wrath . . ." Doing that, you submit to their need to be valued and treated with respect, even when punishing them.

So, again, it is the same type of thing. Children are to submit to parents for the *order* in the family. Parents are to submit to the training needs of children. That can be easily misinterpreted as tolerating their bad behavior, which is not what it means.

For example, suppose a child is in a temper tantrum. It is easier for the parents to demand submission of the child to change that bad behavior. That would be using submission to maintain *order*. "I am the parent, submit to my authority" is an acceptable approach and may be the best approach for that situation. But it is easy to follow that approach without considering how to help the child develop more self-control next time.

The other option would be to use mutual submission, or *harmony*, approach. That means the parent submits to the child's need to develop their self-control. They devote additional time working with the child at that moment to help them change their behavior without the parent using anger, pettiness, manipulation, and unreasonable demands. These types of things create more rebellion in children than obedience.

So the parent puts themselves *under* the child to try to lift them up to higher standards and behavior, serving the child. As opposed to only putting themselves *over* the child and calling the children to put themselves *under* the parent. The first would be a *harmony,* or a mutual submission, approach and the second would be an *order,* or an authority and submission approach.

Submission at Work and Church

The identical situations occur at work and church.

Personally, I was a poor example of submission. I typically talked about how the work was not going right, and I knew a better way to do it, how the authorities in government are so messed up and I knew a better way for them to operate. That is not submission. What I was saying might have been true, but there is a different way to handle these types of things. You are not modeling how submission works when you act as I just described.

So, in work, it is the same type of thing: servants and masters, employee and employer. Ephesians 6:5-8, servants are to submit to the master. And the master is to submit to the servant by not doing them wrong, or paying them fair wages for the work they do. And even if the master is unreasonable, 1 Peter chapter 2:18 tells the servant to honor the master.

So, we easily see the submission of a servant to a master. We, again, do not typically think about the master to the servant. The master to the servant is to submit to the servant's need to be treated properly.

And then, finally, the same type of thing works in the church. Every relationship in the church should have this mutual component. We should be submitting to each other's needs, seeking the best for each other, serving each other, fighting for the place of servanthood, not for the place of taking control.

Submission works in all relationships. All relationships should have this mutuality. The entire church submits to one another in the fear of God.

. . . submitting to one another in the fear of God.

Ephesians 5:21, NKJV

So we not only see submission in marriage, but we also see it in family relationships, work, and church. It is in all of life. That is where we're supposed to be using this mutual submission.

Mutual Submission Scenarios

In each scenario below identify opportunities for mutual submission.

Alejandro and Emilia

Alejandro and Emilia were college sweethearts and now at 25 have been married for 2 years. The marriage has been quite an adjustment for them because both are independent personalities and have succeeded in business early in their careers. Alejandro works in insurance sales and Emilia is a private banker in a large regional bank. They talked about having children, but Emilia is concerned about what she might have to give up if they have kids.

Alejandro was raised in Christian home, where his mother always stayed home and took care of his two brothers and him. His father was a very proud self-made man who came from humble beginnings but worked very hard to support his family, provide security for his wife and kids, and provide a good life for them. He was also a harsh disciplinarian, hoping to teach his boys to stay in line and not get in trouble. Alejandro has a bit of a blind spot in Emilia's eyes, because he doesn't see any of his father's traits in himself.

Emilia and her sister were raised by a pastor and a teacher. Their dad worked as a lead pastor in a small Methodist church and their mom worked at a local elementary school. Both worked to support the family during the girls' years growing up. Emilia always wanted to work outside of the home the way her mother did, because domestic duties always bored her. A straight-A student, Emelia always excelled in school and wanted to apply her education to work.

Here's a recent conversation between Alejandro and Emilia that occurred during their dinner meal. Emilia left work at 5:00 in order to get home and make dinner for two of them.

"How was your day today?" Emilia asked dutifully.

"Tiring, a lot of driving to appointments, and" he paused for dramatic effect, "I made three big sales," he said as he straightened up in his chair.

"I worked really hard today too! I had non-stop appointments with grizzly customers, who don't respect me. At least you don't have to deal with that!"

"Well, everyone isn't nice to me, either. Most people hate insurance salesmen. I'm just trying to make sure I can support you, it's my duty to take care of you and our family."

Emilia rolled her eyes and said, "It's not like I'm a bump on a log and can't earn a living."

"I didn't mean it that way. I just hope that when we have children, you can home-school them. You would be such a great teacher. I feel responsible to build up our savings right now so we can live on one income."

"Thanks for planning my life out for me," she said sarcastically.

Alejandro looked at her but decided anything he said might not go over well. He changed the subject to the new church they were attending since they both like the pastor. When Alejandro was finished, he got up from the table and left his dishes there for Emilia to clean up.

"I have to run an errand to pick up some stuff for an office event tomorrow," he said as he picked up his keys and left.

"See you later," Emilia said with little emotion as she cleared the table and started to clean up the kitchen.

Scenario Questions

1. What opportunities do you see for mutual submission in this scenario?

    _____

    _____

    _____

2. What impacts do you see on attitudes toward submission based on how Emilia and Alejandro were each raised?

    _____

    _____

    _____

The Jordan Family

Andy and Florence have been married for 20 years. They have three children, Hanson, 17 years old, Mary Ann, 15 years old, and April, 8 years old. Hanson recently got his driver's license and now drives, taking his sister Mary Ann to high school every day. Hanson has a speedy two-door car that his dad's brother gave them. Andy and Florence have both warned Hanson about not driving too fast. Andy has warned him that if he gets a ticket there will be consequences. Florence will not let him take April anywhere since she is so young, and she doesn't want April to distract his driving, because she talks a lot. Hanson is responsible to taking Mary Ann to all her before-school and after school activities.

Now that Hanson is driving, Andy is making him work after school at a local grocery store to make sure he understands the privilege of having his own car to drive. One Saturday, Hanson decides he wants to go for a drive in the country. He gets up early and leaves a note for his parents on the kitchen table, saying he is going for a drive in the country to help a friend on a nearby farm.

When Andy and Florence wake up, they call him on his cell phone to get him to come back home because they have a bunch of errands they need him to run for them.

Hanson doesn't pick up because he's driving. When he stops at a gas station to buy a Gatorade, he texts them back saying he won't be home until noon. Andy is furious and goes into a tirade about how selfish Hanson is acting. He texts Hanson back and tells him to come home immediately, *or else*. Hanson replies that he has to pay for his own gas to run all their errands, so he doesn't see why it's a problem for him to take the car for a few hours. He says at least he told them where he was going, which his friends don't have to do.

Florence tells Andy he is overreacting and that he should just calm down. Andy retorts that she is trying to protect him too much. Andy wants to teach him to be a responsible man, who helps others when they need it. Florence reminds him that Hanson went to help the friend on their farm. Andy gets frustrated and says, "Well, we need his help! We are the ones paying for the groceries!"

By this time, it's 10:30am, so Andy just figures he will deal with Hanson when he gets home.

Scenario Questions

1. What opportunities do you see for mutual submission in this scenario?

_____

_____

_____

_____

2.   What changes in the family dynamic could each parent make to build an environment of mutual submission?

_____

_____

_____

_____

All Saints Church

All Saints is a suburban Christian church north of Houston, Texas. Membership has exploded in the last three years since the new young pastor, Nick Alliance, has been there. Nick recognized a need for middle and high school students to connect in a Christian environment in the growing suburb, as families move away from the hustle and bustle of the city. Through their online services they have even drawn members from south of Houston and neighboring towns because the youth program is so strong. Much of the identity of the church is driven by Nick's infectious personality and fun-loving spirit. The church sponsors a lot of retreats, and has engaged the business community in sponsoring events to keep kids out of trouble. Some businesses have even started Bible studies that meet on site in the break room.

Nick is 29 and never married because of his devotion to ministry. He was a college football player with the can-do attitude to defeat any team or giant bigger than he is.

The church has a group of elders who range in age from 40-80. The elder Jamison Harris has been around the church for many years. He is the soft spoken 80-year-old, who doesn't say much in meetings but is always listening attentively. When he does say something, it is always a wise word.

Jamison and his wife Mable have been members of the church since its founding. They discuss the changes they see quite often, as they are concerned that the congregation and teaching is adopting some current-day attitudes that are not totally scriptural.

Sometimes in meetings Nick will say something like, "Old time religion is awesome, but it doesn't always get people in the seats. Youth have been driven away from churches that still play organ music. We need to get them in the door first and show them that God is not a spoilsport."

Other elders are concerned that business leaders who are funding events are looking for too much in return. They say that the business owners are using the church as a form of advertising. Nick's response is, "When I came here, the church was losing money every month. Your last pastor ran away with over $50,000 that he pilfered over the last three years he worked here, and you didn't even know it was missing. I had to do something. I don't think the businesspeople are a problem. They are a part of this community too. This is an innovative program I came up with."

Finally, two of the elders, Joan Ryan, who is a 40-year-old attorney at a small local law firm and Art White, a 50-year-old architect with his own firm, call a meeting of the elders and do not invite Nick. They just feel like the group needs to meet without him because he always interjects his personality and does as he sees fit in spite of what the elders might say. At the meeting, some of the elders did not realize that Nick would not be there. Jamison Harris listens patiently to the points Joan and Art bring up in the meeting. Finally, he says, "It sounds like to me that you two want control of the church back. You feel like Nick has taken something from you."

Joan turns her head toward Art so Jamison can't see her and rolls her eyes as if to say, "The old man doesn't know what he's talking about.

Some of the elders bring up the point that they need to visit with Nick privately, and others feel they should not have had a meeting without him.

Scenario Questions

1. What opportunities do you see for mutual submission in this scenario?

_____

_____

_____

2. What do you think that Nick might need to change?

_____

_____

_____

3. What do you think Joan and Art need to change?

_____

_____

_____

4. What do the other elders need to change?

_____

_____

_____

5. What do Mable and Jamison need to change?

_____

_____

_____

All Star Bar-B-Que

Joyce and Barney Starr, who are brother and sister own All Star Bar-B-Que 50/50 and have built their small bar-b-que stand in their local neighborhood into a hot spot with four locations in their town of 150,000 people. The business has grown exponentially over the past two years and is experiencing growing pains. Barney, the older brother in this scenario is very protective of his younger sister and decides without asking her to hire a COO, James Egbert, to run the business-side of things so they can focus on cooking and serving customers.

Joyce is annoyed that Barney did this because she feels like it will put a dent in their cash flow. She doesn't say anything, because she knows he likes to be in charge of things and is protective of her. At their first meeting with James, the new COO, James hands them a stack of papers an inch thick with all his analysis of what is wrong with the business and why they should close the last two stores they opened. James makes sure to remind them that he has 15 years of accounting experience, and he sees the writing on the wall for the business.

He says, "I left a well-paying job to come help you. I don't want to have to leave in six months because you can't afford to pay me."

Joyce wonders if James looked at their books before he took the position.

Barney chimes in, "James, I think you are a little too worried about business growth. I watched my dad grow the family grocery store business, from one tiny location to three stores. We don't mind working hard to keep all four stores open. It's really too late to go back and close them. Your job is to tell me how we can make it work."

James shakes his head without looking up and says, "I don't know, I don't know."

Joyce says, "Well why don't we have a couple of events in each location where business is the slowest and look at expanding our catering business."

Barney looks at her and smiles in a patronizing way and says, "Good try sis, you are always so optimistic."

Annoyed, she looks at James and says, "Well you're the expert. What do you think?"

The meeting ends awkwardly. Joyce makes an excuse to leave because she thinks Barney hired the wrong person and feels like James is wasting her time. Barney feels like Joyce is naïve about their business because she just knows how to cook food and make people feel welcome.

Scenario Questions

1.   What opportunities do you see for mutual submission in this scenario?

   _____

   _____

   _____

   _____

   _____

2. What do you think that Barney might need to change?

_____

_____

_____

_____

_____

3. What do you think Joyce needs to change?

_____

_____

_____

_____

_____

4. What does James need to change?

_____

_____

_____

_____

_____

REFLECTIVE QUESTIONS

- How does the fear of God relate to mutual submission?

_____

_____

_____

_____

- Why is it important for you to employ mutual submission with your spouse?

_____

_____

_____

_____

- Why is it important for you to employ mutual submission in your family?

_____

_____

_____

_____

- How would employing mutual submission impact your job?

  _____

  _____

  _____

  _____

  _____

- Who do you need to discuss this concept with, in order to improve your relationship with them?

  _____

  _____

  _____

  _____

  _____

SUBMISSION AND AUTHORITY

One of the reasons people struggle with submission and authority is the fact that they look at the world's view of this topic. God's view of authority and leadership is different than what many people think. Our savior Jesus Christ taught his disciples a different view for authority and leadership.

> *Jesus called them together and said, "you know that the rulers of the Gentiles lord it over them, and their high officials exercise authority over them. Not so with you. Instead whoever wants to become great among you must be your servant, and whoever wants to be first must be your slave—just as the Son of Man did not come to be served, but to serve, and to give his life as ransom for many."*

Matthew 20:25-28, NIV

Jesus Christ did not come to be served; He came to serve. He is a perfect example of what *servants leading servants* means. Most leadership focuses on control. The Pharisees thought that way. The Gentile lords, kings, world leaders, presidents of countries and businesses have adopted that view of authority and leadership.

If you look at our society today, you can see plenty of examples of this viewpoint. You want to be great leader? You must have money and power! The more money and power you have, the larger your control and the stronger you will become.

The world most often celebrates men and women with power, fame, and money, so that temptation will always be close to you. You will be tempted to be powerful if you are a leader in your organization or church. You will be tempted to get people to serve you.

Do you want to be great among men, or a faithful servant of God? So, how will you know if you are a Godly leader? Is it because men and women say so? Is it the size of your church or organization, or how much money you manage? How many people you have under you?

You may assume that you are a good leader and use authority correctly because you are a religious leader. Be cautious, because that was the mistake of the Pharisee and scribes, the religious leaders of the day during Jesus Christ's time.

> *Beware of the scribes, who desire to go around*
> *in long robes, love greetings in marketplaces, the*
> *best seats in the synagogues, and the best places*

*at feasts, who devour widows' houses, and for a
pretense make long prayers. These will receive
their condemnation.*

Luke 20:46-47

If you are trying to draw attention to your success
that *you* created as a leader, your mind needs a reset
and renewal. That is not what God wants and it is not
godly thinking. Jesus was the original Servant Leader as
described above in Matthew 20:25-28.

Ask God to renew your mind to be a Servant
Leader under Jesus Christ's authority. When you see
authority and leadership the way God does, your view
of it changes. You can be transformed into the leader
God wants you to be.

Godly Authority Encourages Freedom

Unfortunately, authority is often misused. When
people think or use their *authority* they may do one of
the following:

- Demand justification or evidence.
- State that a person has expert abilities and
  knowledge.
- Demonstrate power to decide.
- Grant freedom for others to act.

While the above are basically positive, do they fit your definition of authority? Do you have a positive view and behavior when you wield authority?

For most people, the answer is no. Authority is constantly misused and creates an image of harshness or abuse. It is also misused when it is seen as a person, meaning the person in charge. Finally, it is misused when the person with the authority minimizes everyone's freedom except their own.

Most dictators around the world misuse the authority they have been given by God and assume they are the authority. But they, like you, are not the authority. You, like Paul, are only a channel or steward of the authority given by God.

> *Let every soul be subject to the governing authorities. For there is no authority except from God, and the authorities that exist are appointed by God.*

> **Romans 13:1, NKJV**

As a leader, you are only a *channel of authority*, a steward of the authority God has given to you. God is the only and ultimate authority over everything, and He uses both good and bad people as channels of His authority in the world.

Let's define authority, understand how God sees authority, and look at the biblical example of the Apostle Paul as a channel of God's authority.

The Greek word for authority is *exousia*, which indicates "freedom of choice." So, a person with great authority has the maximum freedom of choice. On the other hand, the one under authority most often has limited freedom. That is the way it works in the world, but that is not the way God wants His authority used by you. You are His channel of authority.

Since God is the only authority, it is wise to see how He used His authority with us. Here's what Galatians says:

> *Stand fast therefore in the liberty by which Christ has made us free, and do not be entangled again with a yoke of bondage.*

Galatians 5:1, NKJV

God used His authority through the death of Jesus Christ the Son, to set us *free*! That means the example God set for us as channels of His authority is to use authority to provide freedom, not control.

That means authority is definitely not about *ME*. It is not about your position or power. Using authority as God intended means encouraging, even creating, freedom of choice for those you lead and others around you. It does not mean that there are no boundaries or consequences for people who do not follow the rules. Authority used properly allows people to cross the boundaries and experience the consequences, the same way God deals with you.

Godly Authority and Freedom Scenario

In the scenario below make a note of where you see God's authority being used appropriately (encouraging, even creating, freedom of choice for those you lead and others around you), or inappropriately (making it about ME and my position).

Scenario – Leadership Studio, LLC

Alexander Paul and his business partner Julie Anderson are leadership consultants in their newly formed consulting company, Leadership Studio, LLC. They met at a corporate job and decided to free themselves from the toxic environment they were working in.

They landed a new client, Energy Engineering, Inc, that is suffering from growing pains. A number of field leaders from the firm moved to the corporate office, where the corporate infrastructure is burgeoning. Julie landed this contract because the CEO of the company, Jules Ricardo lives next door to Julie and her husband Matt, who is a CPA. Over dinner one night they discussed what was going on with the firm, then Jules convinced the Executive team to hire Leadership Studio, LLC.

As Julie and Alexander (Alex) prepare for the first meeting, this is their conversation.

"Julie, this is really great that we've got this first client, I'm really proud of you for bringing them in."

"You know we are in this 50-50, so of course I'm going to bring in new clients," she said with a smile.

"Oh, I know we are building together, but remember our financial contribution is me at 70 percent and you at 30 percent until you build your book of business," Alex reminded her.

Julie decided not to allow the comment to take her down an unproductive trail, so she didn't say anything.

"I think we will need some junior consultants to help us with this one since the project is so big," Julie said.

"That's true," Alex said. "Who did you have in mind?"

"John Travis just left our old company. He's really good at analyzing situations and has a consultant mindset."

"Consultant mindset?" Alex asked with a quizzical look.

"Meaning he's not one to go into the client and act like he knows everything right off-the-bat. He's good about asking questions to get the client's viewpoint on the situation."

"Okay, I understand," said Alex. "What would the reporting structure be? I trust you Julie, but I have more at stake in this company at this point."

Julie responded, "I thought he would work together with me until I'm sure he can handle it on his own. Then we will both be comfortable with allowing him more freedom in the project."

"Well, let's interview him for the project together. I may have different questions than you do," Alex said. "You know me. I'm particular about the way things are done."

"Sure Alex. Let's look at our calendars to see several times we can offer him to meet."

Alex replied, "Sue (company Admin Assistant) is in charge of my calendar. You can check with her."

Who	Appropriate Use of Authority (encouraging, even creating, freedom of choice for those you lead and others around you)	What they did or said

Who	Inappropriate Use of Authority (made it about ME and my position)	What they did or said

<u>REFLECTIVE QUESTIONS</u>

- As you read the scenario, did you see yourself in the story?

_____

_____

_____

_____

- If you did see yourself, what does it tell you about your attitude toward using authority?

_____

_____

_____

_____

- What do you need to continue doing or stop doing?

_____

_____

_____

_____

Our Power is Unnecessary

When you understand that authority is about freedom and that you are only a channel of God's authority, you can start using God's authority more effectively. Notice how these ideas and principles are demonstrated in Paul's approach with the Corinthian church:

> *I write to those who have sinned before, and to all the rest, that if I come again I will not spare—since you seek a proof of Christ speaking in me, who is not weak toward you, but mighty in you. For though He was crucified in weakness, yet He lives by the power of God. For we also are weak in Him, but we shall live with Him by the power of God toward you.*

1 Corinthians 13:2-4, NKJV

> *I have already warned those who had been sinning when I was there on my second visit. Now I again warn them and all others, just as I did before, that this next time I will not spare them. I will give you all the proof you want that Christ speaks through me. Christ is not weak in his dealings with you; he is a mighty power among you. Although he died on the cross in weakness, he now lives by the mighty power of*

God. We, too, are weak, but we live in him and have God's power—the power we use in dealing with you.

2 Corinthians 13:2-4, NLT

What Paul says here may not be immediately clear, so below is a chart that will help.

The background or context is the Corinthians were questioning Paul's authority. They did not deal with the people who were sinning as Paul had asked, because they did not believe Christ was speaking through Paul to them. They apparently did not believe that Christ was concerned about their sin, so they ignored Paul and, therefore, Christ. They also may have questioned the power of Christ to even deal with their sin.

So Paul states that Christ ". . . is not weak toward you, but mighty in you." In other words, Paul tells them that they do not understand who Christ is and the

perception	reality
Christ does not speak through Paul	(He does, let me prove it to you)
Christ won't deal with our sin	Christ is mightly in you, deals with sin and disobedience.
Christ died on the cross, was weak, not strong	Christ was strong, He won and is alive by the Power of God
Paul is weak, so we do not need to listen to him	Yes, we are weak just like Christ!
Paul has no power	We will use God's power when dealing with you

Therefore, "I will not spare you" = "God will not spare you."

power that He has. He goes on to say (and I paraphrase) "Yes, He died on the cross, which may appear that He was weak, not strong, but you are missing the power of God that raised Christ from the dead and that now He lives by the power of God."

So far, this is a good lesson for leaders to correct errors when noticed. Leaders are called to share the truth but are not responsible for the change in people's lives.

Now it gets even better! Since the Corinthians were mistaken about the power of Christ, they were also mistaken about the power of Christ that was directed at them through Paul. So, here's my wording of what Paul says,

> *"Since you are mistaken about Christ – He is not weak, He is extremely powerful. So, you might say, I am weak, just like Christ is weak! But I do not need to be strong because it is Christ's power that will deal with you. Therefore, when I say, 'I will not spare you', it actually means, God will not spare you. I am not the power; I am just a messenger or channel of the power."*

What an amazing message for leaders who follow Christ! If you rely on your own power, you are doing it completely wrong. Be like Paul. He depended on Christ's authority and power, not his own.

The Power Source Makes the Difference

There is a big difference in the way the world views authority and the way God sees it. The world's view of authority has its roots rigidly attached to *ME*, pride, my position, and my power. Being the power or the authority is the primary focus of your sin nature, which is linked to the world system that is ruled by Satan.

But God's view is drastically different. The roots of authority are deep in God. Authority channels need to value humility because authority is not theirs. It is God's gift or assignment to you. It is not about you; it is about stewardship of God's gift.

Along with that different view of authority comes the big difference in the world's emphasis versus God's. Look at some of the differences below.

World's View	God's View
• "I said"	• "God says"
• *Over*	• *Under*
• Envy	• Content
• Getting	• Giving
• Restricting	• Developing
• Rules and laws	• Grace and freedom
• Being served	• Serving
• Being protected	• Protecting

If you have the world's view, your power source is you and your ability to control others. But God's way is vastly different! Your power source is God who works through you.

A phrase we use when coaching leaders is **"Always find the power from the outside, not from the inside."** That may sound strange, but it means you use the rules, expectations, and values of the organization as the power source. You do not have to act powerful, instead you let the organization's purpose, core values, rules, and expectations be the power.

When those are your power source, you do not need to depend on your persuasiveness or anger to get someone's attention. You simply point them back to those elements, which is the power.

Try this approach and you will notice you have a better attitude when approaching someone needing correction. Why? Because it isn't about you against them or you, the winner. It is about helping them remember what the organization needs from them. Leaders that see themselves only as authority channels for God, become servants of God and people helpers.

Authority is About Developing

When you accept your role as the channel of authority, you can focus on valuing and developing people instead of using your authority to control people. How then do you develop people?

Are you focused on developing people like the Apostle Paul did? Let's see what he says to the Corinthians.

*. . . our authority, which the Lord gave us for
edification and not for your destruction.*

2 Corinthians 10:8, NKJV

*. . . the authority which the Lord has given me
for edification and not for destruction.*

2 Corinthians 13:10, NKJV

Authority is Not About Control

Unfortunately, most leaders are more interested in controlling people rather than developing them. And control does work, you know that because you have done it. You may also know that control works primarily in the short term, relying on fear. If you can maintain a level of fear in people, you can control them until they are brave enough to fight back or rebel.

What control fails to create is self-governance. It can and does create compliance, but nothing more. Control creates a structure where people comply with the minimum requirements, but do not pursue excellence.

Control is a complete misunderstanding about how God wants you to use His authority. Remember that God uses His authority to promote freedom for anyone who wants it.

God gives you the freedom and encourages you to change (2 Peter 1:5). Following Him produces the fruit of the Spirit (Galatians 5:22) which includes self-control, not external control, and that self-control grows when you are accountable for clear expectations and clear consequences.

Godly Authority is Gentle

God's authority is fueled by meekness and gentleness. This is quite the opposite of what the world will tell you. Think about how many management and coaching gurus who work in the business world today, who would never put authority in the same sentence with meekness and gentleness.

> *. . . by the meekness and gentleness of Christ, I appeal to you—I, Paul, who am 'timid' when face to face with you, but 'bold' when away! I beg you that when I come I may not have to be as bold as I expect to be toward some people who think that we live by the standards of this world . . .*

> **2 Corinthians 10:1-2, NKJV**

How clear can Paul be about the proper use of authority? Paul was the conduit, the channel of the authority of God. Jesus is *the* Authority, and He is "meek and gentle" in His dealings with us. His unlimited power is used for our benefit because He is meek and gentle.

That does not mean He is timid! Meekness is best defined as "power under control." Jesus' vast power is not used like the power of a bomb, which is very destructive. Instead, His power is controlled like electricity that powers our lights and other beneficial tools and appliances.

When you use the power of God's authority, you do not try to change people – that is Christ's role. You hope, pray, encourage, exhort, and rebuke, but leave the change up to them and God. That is what Paul did. He was the messenger that things would not go well if they continued to do what Christ stated was sinful and inappropriate behavior.

Notice that Paul did not say anything about his power or authority. He called the Corinthians attention to God's authority, to God's power. Our power is irrelevant and if you do not believe that, you will try to control, instead of call people back to God's standards.

Follows Paul's Example

Passages support this idea that Paul did not try to control the Corinthians, instead he invited them to consider the truth. He did not demand, even though with his position he could have. Why didn't he demand? Because the authority is not Paul's, and he was using Christ's authority in the same way that Christ would use it.

Look at these additional passages and notice that each one is about treating people as Jesus would, with meekness and kindness.

> *Not that we lord it over your faith, but we work with you for your joy.*

2 Corinthians 1:24, NKJV

> *I urge you, therefore to reaffirm your love for Him.*

2 Corinthians 2:8, NKJV

> *Dear friends, purify ourselves from everything that contaminates body and spirit, perfecting holiness out of reverence for God*

2 Corinthians 7:1. NKJV

> *I am not commanding you, but I want to test the sincerity of your love*

2 Corinthians 8:8, NKJV

> *Was it a sin for me to lower myself in order to elevate you?*

2 Corinthians 11:7, NKJV

Here is my advice about what is best for you.

2 Corinthians 11:10, NKJV

Authority is built on the reality of God's Image.

Consider two approaches a leader can take with a person. You can be powerful or relational. The better approach is to use both in the right proportion for any situation.

If you focus on *power*, you distort the image of God, because He is also *relational*. Or, if you think just being relational or getting along is best, you also distort the image of God, because He is also *powerful*.

The reason Paul's example is so good for us to follow, is he used power, but not his power. He used God's power. When you do that, power is used constructively, why? Remember the primary way God uses His power? It is about freeing others, not controlling them. It is about building up, edifying others.

When you use the "power from the outside, not the inside" principle, you use the power of God, not your own power. That frees you to relate to others properly. You do not just try to "get along", because the *power* of God shares the truth with people. So, the table below will help you see that by using God's *power*, you will not distort the image of God. You will tend to relate with power and share truth (power) in love (relate), as it says in Ephesians 4:15.

powerful	relational
• Power comes from God, not us, given, not deserved • Power comes from God's Word to build up, free others, not control • Power of God frees Leaders to *relate*	• Paul related God's power, not his own, as he led • Paul related meekness and gentleness to the people • Paul would not "lord it over your faith" (2 Cor. 1:24) • Paul would "lower myself in order to elevate you" (2 Cor. 11:7)

And it gets even better. The following graphs are designed primarily for marriage, but the same principles apply for leading and discipling others.

Our Perception of Power or Authority

When you think leading is primarily about being served or being in control, your focus is on power. You will try to use God's Word to support your power, your desire to control. You will use the below verses to control people.

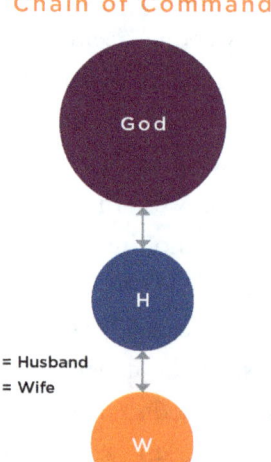

Chain of Command

= Husband
= Wife

> *For the husband is head of the wife, as also Christ is head of the church...*
>
> **Ephesians 5:23, NKJV**

But I want you to know that the head of every man is Christ, the head of woman is man, and the head of Christ is God.

1 Corinthians 11:3, NKJV

God's Reality About Authority

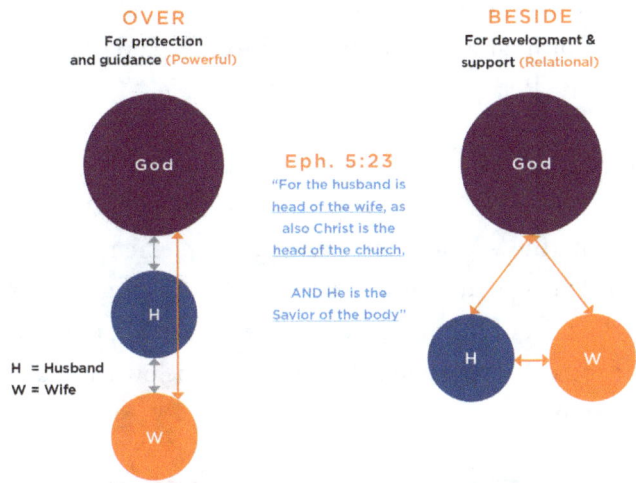

The reality about God's image involves both power and relating. Yes, Ephesians 5:23 is completely true, but what is the purpose of the husband being the head? What is the purpose of the leader being the leader?

It is for *protection* of the followers! That means the power is used *for* the benefit of the wife and followers. Isn't that true of Jesus? He is the All-Powerful God *and*

He is our Savior! Powerful and relational. His power is used *for our* benefit, not His own. Jesus served us with His power. He did not use His power against us.

To summarize the graphics,

The *power* of Authority is from God not us.

Trusting His Power frees leaders to *relate* (Phil. 2:12).

Spiritual authority is *over* for protection and guidance (Powerful).

Spiritual authority is *beside* for development and support (Relational).

Scenario

In the scenario below, identify elements of the world view of authority versus God's view of authority. Make a list of specific actions and nuances you notice in the scenario and which element in the below list that it represents.

World's View	God's View
• "I said"	• "God says"
• *Over*	• *Under*
• Envy	• Content
• Getting	• Giving
• Restricting	• Developing
• Rules and laws	• Grace and freedom
• Being served	• Serving
• Being protected	• Protecting

Edward and Ignacio work at the same School District in a medium-sized town. Edward is the Math Department chair, and Ignacio is Director of the Math curriculum for the District. They are in a Department Meeting with several teachers from different High Schools in the area. Edward and Ignacio called the meeting to get feedback from the teachers regarding the new curriculum they are rolling out. The attendees are June Raymond, who has been teaching Algebra in the District for 2 years at Stellar High School. Since she has joined the school, the awards students have won in UIL Math competitions has skyrocketed based on some time she spent with students after school. George Patterson, from El Capitano High School, has been a Geometry teacher for 15 years. He is a favorite of students and faculty because he makes Geometry fun and experiential. Amy Vault from Eric Campman High School has been teaching Calculus for 5 years. She is known for her high energy and love for Math and students. The school has leveraged her connection with students to get more students to enroll in Calculus in their junior or senior year of High School. Rupert Jones also teaches at El Capitan High School, where he's been a local Math department manager for 2 years. George Patterson reports to him. Rupert teaches a section of Algebra 1 and a section of Algebra II in addition to his administrative duties. Judy Priest has been teaching Math for 30 years. She teaches different subjects each year, due to her lengthy and rich career. She has been offered leadership positions in the District that she always turns down because she wants to stay in the classroom.

Everyone gathers at the District Office at 8:00 am on a Saturday, where Edward and Ignacio greet everyone and offer coffee, juice, water and doughnuts. The meeting begins promptly at 8:15am. Edward distributes an agenda, with specific timeframes for each part of the meeting. He asks that people not interrupt any of the presentations but hold their questions until the end so they can stay on schedule. He says that he wants to get everyone's approval today so he can present the newly approved curriculum to the School Board the following Tuesday evening. He starts his presentation by reading the District by-laws for curriculum changes. Next he introduces Ignacio as his protégé, who hopes will some day advance to his level at the District. He says he very fortunate to have the help of such a hard-working and professional person.

Ignacio's style is a little more laid back than Edward. He starts by thanking everyone for giving up their time on a Saturday and points out a reason that they invited each person to the meeting, based on what they have contributed.

"We are here to serve your needs as teachers, since you are the ones who make our programs come alive. I truly value your expertise and input into the curriculum, so feel free to interrupt me, if there is something we need to discuss in more depth."

He looks at Edward, who is frowning, and says, "Don't worry, we will stay on schedule."

Several people in the room chuckle at the comment.

At the end of Ignacio's presentation, Rupert Jones speaks up about a concern he has with rolling out the new Algebra II curriculum, since he feels like some concepts need to be added to Algebra I, to prepare students to succeed. They all discuss it for about 30 minutes, when Edward says they need to table the conversation for now and move to the next topic.

Rupert is next on the agenda and asks George Patterson to present his presentation on some changes that need to be made to the geometry curriculum.

"I've asked my colleague George to share his expertise and recommendations for the geometry curriculum. He has served our students tirelessly for 15 years and we a lucky to have him on board with us."

"Thank you, Rupert. As you know I am honored to serve our students and our community."

George makes his presentation, and everyone says they think it's a perfect plan.

Edward says, "Super, I'll see if I can get the school board to approve it."

Edward opens the floor for a 15-minute Q&A and for the group to vote to approve the curriculum. Three of the people in the room, say they think adjustments should be made and that they should postpone getting it approved by the school board on Tuesday.

Edward says, "We just don't have time for that. We have to get all this going so we can get funding for new materials and get them ordered in time for the next semester. I've also hired a consultant to help us put finishing touches on the curriculum materials. If you want to make changes or think about something, we'll have to reconvene in a Zoom call on Monday."

Everyone agrees that they will take more time out of their weekend to make sure that what is presented and approved by the school board is the best option for students.

The Zoom meeting is set, and the meeting is adjourned.

Make note of which elements of the two views of authority you noted from the scenario.

World View

Element	Person	What they did or said

God's View

Element	Person	What they did or said

REFLECTIVE QUESTIONS

- Think about your view of authority in your relationships. Do you have issues with control that you need to change?

_____

_____

_____

_____

- Considering the graph below, reflect on how your view your relationship with your spouse. Are you focused more on the OVER graph or the BESIDE? Based on your assessment, what do you need to continue or improve on?

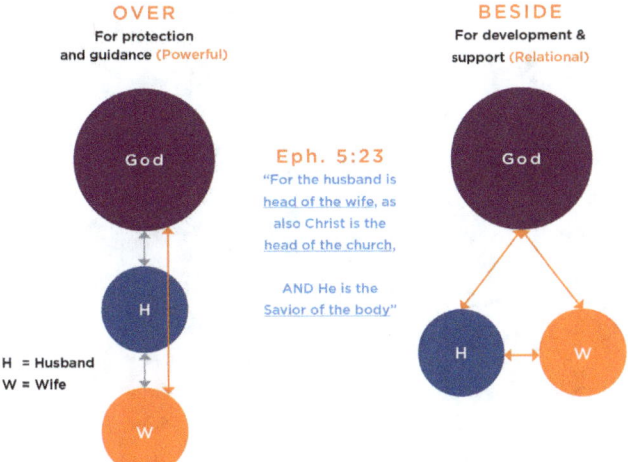

OVER
For protection and guidance (Powerful)

Eph. 5:23
"For the husband is head of the wife, as also Christ is the head of the church,

AND He is the Savior of the body"

BESIDE
For development & support (Relational)

God

H

W

H = Husband
W = Wife

_____

_____

_____

_____

- What do you need to do to trust God's power
  more than you trust your own power? How will
  this impact your relationship with God and
  with those around you?

TRUE LEADERSHIP

God asks leaders to use His authority correctly by freeing people, being gentle, and serving others. Doing those three things will result in leading correctly. Leaders should be servants not dictators and when people employ godly authority, they can lead others the way God wants them to.

As a reminder, leadership is misunderstood. All of the attention is focused on the leader. The world's view of leadership is self-absorbed. That creates a bad leadership structure. If people aren't doing what you want, you will become defensive and let them know you are the boss, the top dog, the leader.

When you try to prove you are the leader, most often you are no longer leading. You are a dictator and worse, you are reacting and responding, not leading.

Leadership is not about you! Leadership is about serving.

The list below describes some attributes of true Servant Leaders:

- They follow God the true leader, doing what He says is right and best and are not dependent on or trying to please followers or others.

- They think about their relationship with God first and consider followers and others second.
- They value followers enough to spend energy developing them and invite, encourage followers to self-governance.
- They understand and share the *Truth* on which they stand and relate or offer the *Truth* to followers and others who decide to follow.
- They focus on There, Here, and Path and invite others to go There, see Here and walk (act, learn, adjust on) the Path.

There, Here, Path

This concept was described with more detail in the book entitled, *Did You Choose the Right Path?* from this series. Since it is a critical concept for true leadership, here is a synopsis. The graphic below gives you a visual of what this concept represents.

You use your car to get somewhere, a desired destination. When you start the "journey" from your home for example, you have to know your starting point. So, to get from here, your home, to your destination, you have a path of action steps to make that happen. So, applying this to leadership, you have a destination that you and your team, which may be your

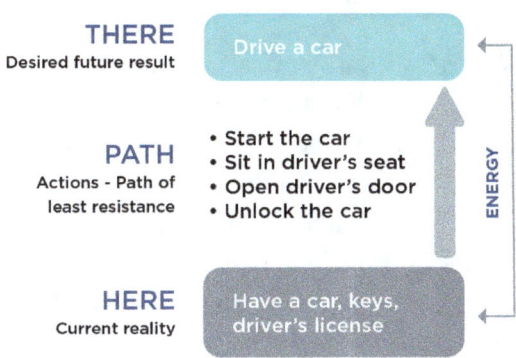

spouse, your family, a church or work group, want to get to. That destination needs to be clearly defined. Where you are now also needs to be clearly defined. Then, the steps or Path between Here and There can be clearly articulated.

So, as a leader make sure you have the *There,* where you want to go, and the *Here*, where you are now clearly articulated to you and whoever you are leading. With those two clear points, you can more easily define the next actions to take on the *Path*.

In my years of working with people, companies, and myself, these three problems show up often. Yes, there are more problems than this, but these three capture the essence of the struggle.

- Rudderless
- Blind
- Unfocused

Rudderless means a lack of clarity about purpose, strategy, and goals. You are unclear of where you are going. You are just like the question, "What is the difference between a ship without rudder and a captain without a charted course? Nothing! Both will go somewhere driven by the currents, wind, and tide of the day."

Or you may be *Blind*. That means you are not in touch with reality, "how things really are". The actual state of the organization or your life is unclear. When people are unclear about their current reality, they tend to fall into two fallacies. Believing that things are *better* than they really are, or they are *worse* than they really are. They become subjective, not objective about life. They editorialize and estimate and guess and speculate rather than just observe reality.

Finally, *Unfocused* is most often the result of the first two, but it can also happen by ignoring a clear end result and current reality. Your days, weeks, and months are filled with inconsistent and uncoordinated actions. Your life is filled with "fighting brush fires". While often remarkably busy, there is little to show for your work and effort.

The graphic depicts how you should be using There, Here and the Path (THP) to lead others. The solution using THP is as logical as you trying to drive to a destination in your car. You have to be crystal clear about your destination and your current location, then your Path is a matter of connecting Here to There.

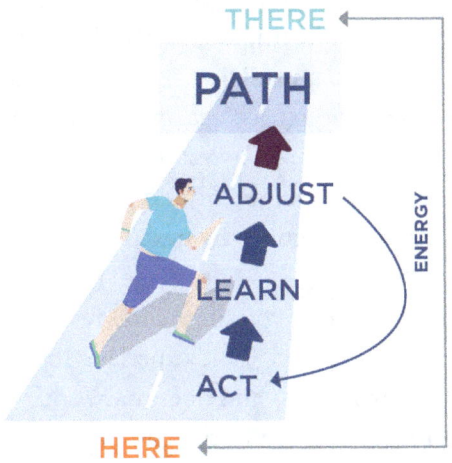

The difference when leading people comes with executing the Path from Here to There. With people, you must take action and learn from each action as you travel the *Path*. It is an iterative process.

Act, Learn, Adjust

> *Action without reflection is mindless.*

Henry Mintzberg, Canadian Author on Business and Management

The creative process is not a manufacturing process. Other people may have done what you are trying to do, but you have not done it. That means you are trying to create something new, at least for you.

While the creative process has the engine of THP, it is fueled by Act, Learn, Adjust (ALA) once you start on the PATH. Because it is the creative process, you want to LEARN from each action as you execute.

- Act—Look at the result of the action.
- Learn—Did it help? Did it hurt?
- Adjust or act on the next step.

Using ALA helps you do the following.
- Gain knowledge and experience by acting.
- See what does and does not work.
- Revise plans to fit the current situation.
- Keep moving toward the Result—one Action at a time.

When things are not working, you learn to ask the question, "What are we learning?"

THP is the beginning of the Creative Process that Robert Fritz teaches. The process has been around for thousands of years and is the foundation for most things that are created or done. Your brain is actually wired for THP, you can now become disciplined to follow the process.

This quote from Abraham Lincoln that shows that he was using the structure:

If we could first know there we are, and whither
we are tending, we could better judge what to do,
and how to do it.

Get yourself focused by first determining your THERE, then your HERE, and finally develop some actions to move you along the PATH. Only then can you get others to follow you.

THP can be a really great tool for you as a leader.

There, Here, Path Scenario

In the scenario below look for the following ineffective elements (blind, rudderless, unfocused) and positive elements (Act, Learn, Adjust).

Scenario—Save the Children

Hubert Chang grew up poor and he and his family often had to skip meals because they did not have enough money. Hubert is the oldest of eight children, and the first one in his family to attend college. Now at 55, in the second half of his life, he wants to do something to help others who suffered as he did.

Hubert sets up a 501(c)3 non-profit to feed hungry children. An influencer-type of personality, he gets six of his friends and business colleagues to join him in his quest to help poor people.

They convene the first meeting on a Wednesday evening. The group includes the following people.

- Emilio Prince – 50, deacon at the church Hubert attends, Marketing Director of a mid-sized company.
- Samantha Stone – 45, Stay-at-home-Mom who lives next door to Hubert and his family.
- Susan Ahn – 55, business colleague of Hubert, legal counsel for the company she and Hubert work for.
- David Wilson—35, CPA, Hubert's neighbor.
- Tina Gordon—55, Publisher, attends same church as Hubert and his family.
- Ivan Slovensky—40, Pastor of the church Hubert and his family attend.
- Clara Weinstein—65, Retired teacher, who is friends with Hubert's wife.
- Ed Harrington—55, Real Estate Attorney, a college friend of Hubert's.

Hubert kicks off the meeting by thanking everyone for attending. He says, "You are helping me achieve something that's on my bucket list. I can't tell you how much I appreciate you doing this."

David asks, "Do we have an agenda, so we can stay on track with the meeting?"

Hubert replies, "Oh, I didn't think of that. I don't expect this meeting to go very long."

Hubert continues, "First of all, I want us to think of a catchy name, that will draw donors and volunteers."

Emilio asks, "Who is the target of people we are helping?"

"Hungry kids," Hubert answers.

Emilio continues, "Okay, who are you thinking that is? Kids in our town, our state, our nation?"

Hubert says, "I never really thought about that, but what do you guys think?"

Susan says, "Well I think we need to get a true vision of what we are trying to do and who exactly we are trying to help. We can't hit the mark if we don't have a target."

Clara, Tina, and Ivan nod their heads in agreement.

Hubert says, "Let's start with our town. We don't have much seed money, so we need to start small. If we only feed one needy family a year, that is fine with me. So, let's think of a name, so we can get seed money to get started."

"Who do you see as primary donors?" Emilio asks.

"I thought business owners and professionals, because they are always looking for tax write-offs."

"You have to find people who are interested in your cause. I have at least three requests for donations a week," Ed says. "People think that because I'm an attorney, I have piles of money I'm sitting on, ready to give away."

David says, "Look, let's start at the beginning. Let's write a simple vision and mission statement first, then we can build on that foundation. Once we have that, we can begin to build a plan of action."

"Right," Samantha says. "Before I retired from working to have kids, I grew my business as a physical therapist by first figuring out where my clients were. Meaning, are they athletes, elders, or people who get injured because they pushed it too hard at the gym. From that I made a plan to grow the business. Some things I implemented didn't work, so I would figure out why it didn't work, then adjust it, or throw it out altogether."

Hubert says, "Thank you for sharing that, Samantha. That makes a lot of sense."

Some of the people in the room were a little impatient because they felt like Hubert was not prepared for the kickoff meeting.

Susan suggested, "Hubert, why don't we reconvene, when you are more clear about exactly what you are trying to accomplish. I'm glad to help you virtually before we meet again."

Several people chimed in and agreed with Susan.

Hubert said, "Thank you all for attending this evening. I will send out an email for next steps for those who still want to participate. We will meet again in the next 60 days or so."

Everyone said their good-byes and left the meeting.

Looking through the scenario, complete the chart below.

Poor Execution of THP

Element - Rudderless, blind, unfocused	Person	What they did or said

Appropriate Execution (description) of THP

Element - Act, learn, adjust	Person	What they did or said

REFLECTIVE QUESTIONS

- Think of a time when you needed to use THP as a leader. Identify what you did well and what you need to change.

- When you are in a group and someone else is leading, what can you do to help them use THP more effectively?

Leaders Don't Have to Lead

If you think you *should, must,* or *have to* lead, you will create a big problem for yourself and the people you lead. At minimum, you will decrease your energy to lead, because you are doing it from obligation, not want.

If you lead, because you *have to*, then you will probably have a bad attitude and expect others to show their appreciation for what you do. Satan wants you to have that attitude, because he knows you are focused on yourself and not others. You have made a choice to lead or not, but not because you think you *have to*.

Service Above Self

General Schwarzkopf makes a poignant point about service above self in his book:

> *"The Army, with its emphasis on rank and medals and efficiency reports, is the easiest institution in the world in which to get consumed with ambition. Some officers spend all their time currying favor and worrying about the next promotion — a miserable way to live. But West Point saved me from that by instilling the ideal of service above self — to do my duty for my country even if it brought no gain at all. It gave me far more than a military career — it gave me a calling."*

It Doesn't Take a Hero, **General H. Norman Schwarzkopf**

Paul's Leadership Style

Here is a summary of Paul's leadership style as shown in 2 Corinthians 11. Review this and reflect on your own leaderships to see if you are aligned with how Jesus would lead.

- Cares deeply for and identifies with those he led (verses 1–2).
    - ○ *Oh, that you would bear with me in a little folly—and indeed you do bear with me. 2 For I am jealous for you with godly jealousy. For I have betrothed you to one husband, that I may present you as a chaste virgin to Christ.*

- Offers protection to & exhorts those he led (verses 3-4, 12-15).
    - ○ *3 But I fear, lest somehow, as the serpent deceived Eve by his craftiness, so your minds may be corrupted from the simplicity that is in Christ. 4 For if he who comes preaches another Jesus whom we have not preached, or if you receive a different spirit which you have not received, or a different gospel which you have not accepted—you may well put up with it.*
    - ○ *12 But what I do, I will also continue to do, that I may cut off the opportunity from those who desire an opportunity to be regarded*

just as we are in the things of which they boast. 13 For such are false apostles, deceitful workers, transforming themselves into apostles of Christ. 14 And no wonder! For Satan himself transforms himself into an angel of light. 15 Therefore it is no great thing if his ministers also transform themselves into ministers of righteousness, whose end will be according to their works.

- Speaks in an unwavering and sober manner about abilities and position (verses 5-6).
  - *5 For I consider that I am not at all inferior to the most eminent apostles. 6 Even though I am untrained in speech, yet I am not in knowledge. But we have been thoroughly manifested among you in all things.*
  - Defends position and ministry, but not himself; (he is not defensive, or about ME).

- Refuses to be a burden or dependent on those he led (verses 7–11).
  - *7 Did I commit sin in humbling myself that you might be exalted, because I preached the gospel of God to you free of charge? 8 I robbed other churches, taking wages from them to minister to you. 9 And when I was present with you, and in need, I was a burden to no one,*

for what I lacked the brethren who came from Macedonia supplied. And in everything I kept myself from being burdensome to you, and so I will keep myself. 10 As the truth of Christ is in me, no one shall stop me from this boasting in the regions of Achaia. 11 Why? Because I do not love you? God knows!

- Speaks the truth, communicates clearly with those he led (verses 16-21).
    - *16 I say again, let no one think me a fool. If otherwise, at least receive me as a fool, that I also may boast a little. 17 What I speak, I speak not according to the Lord, but as it were, foolishly, in this confidence of boasting. 18 Seeing that many boast according to the flesh, I also will boast. 19 For you put up with fools gladly, since you yourselves are wise! 20 For you put up with it if one brings you into bondage, if one devours you, if one takes from you, if one exalts himself, if one strikes you on the face. 21 To our shame I say that we were too weak for that! But in whatever anyone is bold—I speak foolishly—I am bold also.*

- Suffers for those he led (verses 22-27).

    o *22 Are they Hebrews? So am I. Are they
       Israelites? So am I. Are they the seed of Abraham?
       So am I. 23 Are they ministers of Christ?—I
       speak as a fool—I am more: in labors more
       abundant, in stripes above measure, in prisons
       more frequently, in deaths often. 24 From the
       Jews five times I received forty stripes minus
       one. 25 Three times I was beaten with
       rods; once I was stoned; three times I was
       shipwrecked; a night and a day I have been
       in the deep; 26 in journeys often, in perils of
       waters, in perils of robbers, in perils of my own
       countrymen, in perils of the Gentiles, in perils
       in the city, in perils in the wilderness, in perils
       in the sea, in perils among false brethren; 27 in
       weariness and toil, in sleeplessness often, in
       hunger and thirst, in fastings often, in cold and
       nakedness*

- Boasts in and trusts God not himself (verses
  28-31).

    o *28 besides the other things, what comes
       upon me daily: my deep concern for all the
       churches. 29 Who is weak, and I am not
       weak? Who is made to stumble, and I do not
       burn with indignation? 30 If I must boast, I
       will boast in the things which concern my [d]*

infirmity. 31 The God and Father of our Lord Jesus Christ, who is blessed forever, knows that I am not lying.

REFLECTIVE QUESTIONS

- How can you relate this quote to your view of how you lead people in your life?

  "The Army, with its emphasis on rank and medals and efficiency reports, is the easiest institution in the world in which to get consumed with ambition. Some officers spend all their time currying favor and worrying about the next promotion — a miserable way to live. But West Point saved me from that by instilling the ideal of service above self — to do my duty for my country even if it brought no gain at all. It gave me far more than a military career — it gave me a calling."

  It Doesn't Take a Hero, **General H. Norman Schwarzkopf**

  _____

  _____

  _____

  _____

  _____

  _____

- How can you incorporate the attributes of Paul's leadership style from 2 Corinthians 11 into your life?

    ○ *Cares deeply for and identifies with those he led (verses 1–2).*

    ○ *Offers protection to & exhorts those he led (verses 3-4, 12-15.)*

    ○ *Speaks in an unwavering and sober manner about abilities and position (verses 5-6).*

    ○ *Defends position and ministry, but not himself; (he is not defensive, or about ME).*

    ○ *Refuses to be a burden or dependent on those he led (verses 7–11).*

    ○ *Speaks the truth, communicates clearly with those he led (verses 16-21).*

- What do you need to change in your life and your relationships to become a true leader?

  _____

  _____

  _____

  _____

  _____

  _____

STUDY GUIDE

Scripture Meditation

Time: 30 minutes a day

Each day read and meditate on one of the scriptures listed below or as directed by your session leader.

Follow these steps.

1. Get in a quiet place without distraction.
2. Play a praise song, and just listen to the words.
3. Ask God to reveal His heart and meaning to you as you read the scriptures.
4. Write your reflections below or in your journal.
5. Read the scriptures daily so you receive maximum revelation.

Ephesians 5:18-21, NKJV	Isaiah 57:15, NKJV	Ezekiel 1:26, NKJV
James 4:1, NKJV	Ephesians 5:22-31, NKJV	Ephesians 6:1-4, NKJV
Ephesians 6:5-9, NKJV	Matthew 20:25-28, NIV	Philippians 2:12, NIV
Romans 13:1, NKJV	2 Corinthians 11, NKJV	Ephesians 5:23, NKJV

REFLECTIVE QUESTIONS

1. Why is submission so important in our relationships among each other and our relationship with God?

    _____

    _____

    _____

2. If we could all learn to follow Ephesians 5:21, how would it positively impact society, our local communities, and our families?

    _____

    _____

    _____

3. Think of some relationships in your life that are not working. How could submitting to each other improve those relationships? What specifically will you do differently in those relationships to improve them? For example, listen to other's opinions and show a higher level of respect for their ideas?

    _____

    _____

    _____

4. How do you need to change your perspective
    on authority and leadership to reflect what
    God had in mind concerning these topics?

_____

_____

_____

5. How can you apply Paul's leadership style
    to your life? How will this impact you
    relationships in all different areas of your life?

_____

_____

_____

6. Since reading this book, how has your
    perspective on Ephesians 5:23 changed?

_____

_____

_____

7. Based on what you have read in this book, do
    you think you are a true leader? If so, describe
    what you do that makes you think that. If not,
    what do you need to improve or change?

_____

_____

_____

TOOLS

Each book in this series has a supplemental video course on www.gr8relate.com/video-courses/ under the heading "BOOK SERIES Video Courses." The videos were selected from the COMPLETE Video Courses to support the book and provide more details. If you want more details than the book offers, use the COMPLETE Video Courses and the GR8 Relationships Study Guide.

The following tools will enable you to understand yourself and your spouse and how you can work together to handle conflict. The videos listed below are a part of the video course that corresponds to the information in this book. Completing all the courses will be instrumental in helping you find FREEDOM!

You can find all these tools and many more on our website, www.gr8relate.com, on the TOOLS tab.

Kolbe Assessment https://gr8relate.com/kolbe

You can trust the validity and accuracy of the Kolbe instrument to show you your strengths and instincts. The Kolbe also helps you easily see and understand how the strengths and talents of one person may not be considered as strengths by another. This critical information will help you bridge the gap between reality and your expectations of them. Once you complete the assessment, you will receive detailed reports that will help you understand your strengths and talents and how to use your strengths in a complementary way with your spouse, family member, or friend's strengths. By understanding your instincts, you can more easily discuss your differences, laugh about them and develop ways to deal with them.

The Thomas-Kilman Conflict Mode Instrument (TKI)   https://gr8relate.com/tki

The TKI is the world's best-selling instrument for understanding conflict. It helps you see that conflict can be beneficial and useful instead of thinking conflict as bad. You will be provided detailed information on effectively using all five conflict modes—competing, collaborating, compromising, avoiding, and accommodating.

The Fundamental Interpersonal Relations Orientation-Behavior™ (FIRO-B®). https://gr8relate.com/firob

The FIRO-B helps you understand how you interact at work and personal life. This easy-to-complete assessment will provide critical insights into how an individual interacts with others. This personality instrument measures how you typically behave with others and how you expect them to act toward you.

Individual Videos

We have a FREE video course that corresponds with the information in this book.

These are short courses that you can watch/listen at your own pace. Enter the information in parenthesis below into your browser and you will be taken to a video course. When you are online, scroll down and click the "Sign Up / Start Course" button to create an account. You only need an account to access all the free courses.

There are two options:

- BOOK SERIES Courses: Each book in the GR8 Relationships series will have a video course with specific videos selected from the COMPLETE Courses that help explain the contents of the book. This book's video course is below.
  - *The S Word (https://gr8relate.com/ video-courses/the-s-word/)*
- COMPLETE Courses: These are the original, complete courses that give you more details about the information in this book.

o *09A – The "S" Word - Submission (https://gr8relate.com/video-courses/s-word-submission/)*

o *09B – Authority and Leadership – Paul's Example (https://gr8relate.com/video-courses/authority-and-leadership-pauls-example/)*

o *12B – Creating the Relationship You Want (https://gr8relate.com/video-courses/creating-the-relationship-you-want/)*

TWO CIRCLES

1. _____ / _____   1. _____ / _____
2. _____   2. _____
3. _____   3. _____

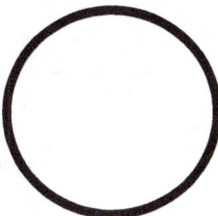

The PROBLEM and 4 Mistakes

The PROBLEM – Make Everything about ME

- Take everything personally by making your "ME" flash
- Live only by appetites, impulses, and pleasures
- Don't think— react/respond to everything emotionally
- Be happy, satisfied, and content only if people and circumstances are treating you right
- Only consider others when there is something in it for YOU.

> **James 3:16** – Where envy and self-seeking exist, confusion and every evil thing are there.
> **Philippians 2:3** – Let nothing be done through selfish ambition or conceit, but in lowliness of mind let each esteem others better than himself.

Operate on Opinion and Emotions – **The POLITICIAN**

- When we can't find or don't know the facts – we tend to "fill in the blanks"
- Opinion = judgment or belief not founded on certainty or proof; seem to be true or probable
- Emotions are RESPONDERS and often UNTRUSTWORTHY
- Objectivity = How it IS
- Subjectivity = How it FEELS
- "Who is my "who-said-so"?

> **Judges 21:25** – In those days there was no king in Israel; everyone did what was right in his own eyes.
> **Proverbs 3:5-6** – Trust in the LORD with all your heart, and lean not on your own understanding; in all your ways acknowledge Him, and He shall direct your paths

Keep the Past in the Present – **The VICTIM**

- Do not understand the power of forgiveness
- Do not understand the power of confession
- Do not understand that the PAST IS OVER
- Do not understand you are being controlled
- Good relationships leave a trail of resolved issues

> **Luke 17:3** – And if he sins against you seven times in a day, and seven times in a day returns to you, saying, 'I repent,' you shall forgive him.
> **1 John 1:9** – If we confess our sins, He is faithful and just to forgive us our sins and to cleanse us from all unrighteousness.

Wear a Mask – **The ACTOR**

- Acting or pretending, not being a REAL person
- "Walking on eggshells," dance around problems
- Not willing to seek or share the truth
- IMPLIES – I'm free to lie, but not free to tell the truth
- It takes 2 REAL people to have a REAL relationship

> **Ephesians 4:15** – …but, speaking the truth in love, may grow up in all things into Him who is the head— Christ

Try to Change Others – **The DICTATOR**

- You think others should never be free to choose their path because they will mess things up
- You believe that other people must change to be like you want them
- You assign them a "JOB" to make you happy
- Reality is that the heart of a relationship is to know others for who they are and still accept, value, and love them.

> **Galatians 5:1** – Stand fast therefore in the liberty by which Christ has made us free, and do not be entangled again with a yoke of bondage.
> **Galatians 5:13** – For you, brethren, have been called to liberty; only do not use liberty as an opportunity for the flesh, but through love serve one another.

Pursuing their BEST
— in Work, In Life, At Love

THP Personal Planning Form

1. THERE—Goals, Desired Outcomes (Picturable, Measurable, Specific)		Due Date	

2. HERE—Current Reality	

3. PATH—Actions	Progress Measures	Partners	Date

Date Prepared:	Approved by:

242 Spring Park Drive, Ste A   Midland, Texas 79705   Phone: 432-682-6823   https://gr8relate.com   Email: info.gr8relate@gr8grp.com

Focus Triangle

Instructions

1. List items that you need to do in the **INTEND** section. Use the back for more.
2. Review the INTEND list and write 1 to 3 that you commit to do today in the **COMMIT** section.
3. Review the INTEND list and write up to 6 items you will ATTEMPT to do today.
4. All other items stay on your INTEND list to be reviewed tomorrow or in the near future.

COMMIT

ATTEMPT

INTEND

Ten Steps to Your Best Relationships!

Do you desire to have better, healthier relationships? Do you find that on some days, it seems like a struggle? If so, you are not alone. Here are ten steps that can lead you to experience your best relationships ever.

Step 1. Study God's Design for Excellent Relationships

The design of a butter knife lets you know that it works best when spreading soft things like room-temperature butter. If you try to use it to cut a T-bone steak, you will see that it is not designed to do that. The same is true for excellent relationships.

God had a clear purpose and design when He created man and woman. He designed man to be different from a woman so that the two would not only be complimentary but, more importantly, display His image to a lost and dying world.

Step 2. Recognize How Men and Women Are Different - REALLY!

God created man and woman perfectly to fulfill their designed roles which complement each other.

If you remember, God created Eve because He did not want Adam alone. Without a woman, man has no one to help "fill the earth and subdue it" (Gen 1:28). Adam needed a suitable helper to fulfill God's purpose for mankind. And for a woman, it is imperative to remember that Helper is a word used primarily about God (i.e., Ps 121:1-2), further elevating rather than demeaning women.

God designed a woman to fulfill a relational role while a man fulfills his work role design – the differences are complementary, not conflicting.

Step 3. Accept the ONE PROBLEM!

Did you know that there is only ONE PROBLEM?

Making everything about ME is THE PROBLEM that destroys relationships. It is the root from which relationship mistakes grow. Unfortunately, we are blind to how often we make life about ME! You may have noticed how easy it is to see when others are being selfish and self-absorbed, but not when you are doing it.

When others are making life about ME, it's like they have this big ME on their forehead. They cannot see it – because it is on their forehead above their eyes! The same is true for you; they see it!

Step 4. Discover the Unknown Judgments for Men and Women

Every woman and man that has, is, and will live is subject to the judgments issued by God. And this affects every relationship.

Understanding these judgments is like unlocking the secrets of what drives and motivates lousy relationships. Learning these profound judgments enables you to identify difficulties and issues in your relationships and see the damage they are creating for you now.

Woman

- **Designed to RELATE:** The woman's unique design helps, nurtures, and supports healthy relationships, especially with her husband and children.
- **RELATING is Judged:** The woman's judgment adds pain to relationships and drives her to control them, which creates more pain, especially with her husband and children.

Man

- **Designed to WORK:** The man's design provides, protects, and preserves others, especially his wife and children.
- **WORK is Judged:** The man's judgment adds pain to work and drives him to control work, which creates more pain, especially for his wife and children.

Step 5. Devote Yourself to the SOLUTION

Would you be happy, or at least more satisfied, if they just changed?

That thinking encourages the PROBLEM, not the SOLUTION. You ignore the changes needed in your li because, after all, "They are the problem, not me..."

The Solution is the opposite of the Problem. The Solution will *pursue their best patiently, kindly, sacrificially, and unconditionally*. That is a definition of love from God's Word. God asks us to have "lowliness of mind to let each esteem others better than himself." (Phil 2:3)

When you live that definition, you relate to others as God relates to us. So, spend energy making changes *God wants you to make* and release the other person to God.

Love does not focus on ME or judge or complain about people, especially those near you. Love does r try to get others to help you change difficult people. Love never manipulates or dominates others to make you feel better. Instead, love always promises, promotes, and provides freedom for others to relate to you or not because it focuses on the best for others.

Step 6. Learn How Your Feelings Work

Great relationships depend on effectively understanding the link between thinking, feeling, acting, ar the Solution. If you do not see how your emotions are always responding and are often untrustworth then you will not see how it can be dangerous to "follow your heart."

Please understand emotions or feelings are not bad, and you must become emotionless—quite the opposite. Your emotions are God-given but know that you can control them.

Step 7. Choose the Reality of Freedom

Freedom is "not controlling or being controlled." It dramatically changes relationships, yet it is not the most crucial element for superior relationships. Relationships will suffer from irresponsible freedom i freedom is not underneath the Solution. Choose wisely!

Remember, love is the Solution, and *pursues their best patiently, kindly, sacrificially, and unconditiona* It takes your freedom to a higher standard, always responsible, never irresponsible (which limits your freedom). Love sets and respects boundaries; freedom without love is irresponsible and ignores boundaries. When your ME is flashing, it uses your freedom irresponsibly.

Step 8. Remove Bitterness, Resentment, and Grudges

Forgiveness removes bitterness, resentment, and grudges. It is the only way to get free from the harr others have done to you. Seriously, the only way!

It requires courage and trust in a PERFECT Father God to use it. There are severe consequences for yc and your relationships when you do not forgive.

When you forgive, the result is freedom from being controlled by a past event or person that has harmed you.

Step 9. Confess. Deal with Real and False Guilt

Like forgiveness, superior relationships also need confession. Without those two, you have no cure for the pain of wrongs done to you and wrongs you do to others. Both are necessary to stop being controlled by the past.

Confession is how you deal with real guilt. It prevents you from being controlled by what you have done to others. It is an external act from an internal change of heart. And it is best done first to God, then to the person you harmed.

Because of Satan's constant bombardment of lies, he wants you to feel guilty for things God has not declared wrong. That is false guilt; one clear example occurs when you confess real guilt. Satan starts whispering in your ear, "But you still did it," trying to remove the freedom God grants (1 Jn 1:9). Yes, you did it, but God is no longer paying attention to it.

Step 10. Follow the Path to Transformation

God provided a clear path if you want transformation. God will not make you do the steps He has provided. But, when you start the process, you participate in the abundant life you have been given (2 Pet 1:3). The benefits and promises God states that are part of the abundant life are incredibly appealing. He says...

- you "...have been given...exceedingly great and precious promises" (2 Pet 1:3)
- that through the promises "you may be partakers of the divine nature" (2 Pet 1:4) and
- you have "escaped the corruption that is in this world" (2 Pet 1:4)

While that is incredible, He also reveals three promises if you take the transformation path and one painful, solemn warning if you don't (2 Pet 1:8-9). Start today practicing these steps for transformation.

Hermann Eben is the founder and CEO of GR8 Relationships. To know more, visit https://gr8relate.com/video-courses/). You will find FREE video courses that walk you through God's design. These courses are short and easy to follow and can put you on the path to Pursuing *Their* Best patiently, kindly, sacrificially, and unconditionally.

www.GR8Relate.com